Animal Clues

A game for two or more players

David Drew

RIGBY

How to play

How good is your knowledge of animals?

On each page is a puzzle to solve.

Look carefully at the pictures and read the clues. Can you guess the animal's name?

When you have guessed, turn the page for the answer.

Here is my eye

and here are my claws.

I live near your house.
I am a ...

lizard.

Here is my claw

and here is my shell.

I live at the beach.
I am a ...

crab.

Here is my head

and here are my wings.

I live in the grass.
I am a ...

grasshopper.

Here is my skin

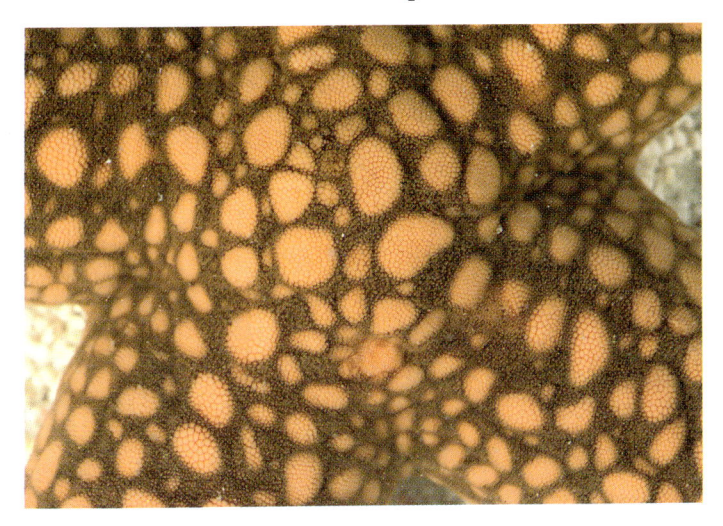

and here is my mouth.

I live in the sea.
I am a ...

sea star.

Here is my eye

and here is my foot.

I live in a pond.
I am a ...

frog.

Here is my tongue

and here is my wing.

I live in your garden.
I am a ...

butterfly.

Here are my eyes

and here is my silk.

I live on the ground.
I am a ...

spider.